THE
Dictionary
WO(FOR)MEN

B. Lyric

ARCHWAY
PUBLISHING

Disclaimer: The definitions and theories presented provide one realistic
example of a particular term. A man may or may not have all the characteristics
of one term or fall into several categories. A woman may or may not live
by a particular theory for other reasons than the examples present.

Archway Publishing books may be ordered
through booksellers or by contacting:

Archway Publishing
1663 Liberty Drive
Bloomington, IN 47403
www.archwaypublishing.com
1 (888) 242-5904

Because of the dynamic nature of the Internet, any web addresses or
links contained in this book may have changed since publication and
may no longer be valid. The views expressed in this work are solely those
of the author and do not necessarily reflect the views of the publisher,
and the publisher hereby disclaims any responsibility for them.

Any people depicted in stock imagery provided by Thinkstock are
models, and such images are being used for illustrative purposes only.
Certain stock imagery © Thinkstock.

ISBN: 978-1-4808-2712-7 (sc)
ISBN: 978-1-4808-2711-0 (hc)
ISBN: 978-1-4808-2713-4 (e)

Library of Congress Control Number: 2016948551

Print information available on the last page.

Archway Publishing rev. date: 10/03/2017

FOREWORD
by Scott Shanks

You might be wondering how a man got involved with popularizing a dictionary meant for women. It was quite by accident. I met the author at a business lunch, and by chance she mentioned that she had written and published her own book about men. Her idea was to just have some fun by interviewing friends, family, and associates about all the dating and relationship experiences they had endured. The book was meant to be a rundown of the different types of men women might meet, the pros and cons of each type, with some relationship advice thrown in for good measure. Curious, I bought the book.

I loved what I read. The book was entertaining, relatable and enlightening. The light-hearted approach suggested by the common slang terms the author devised to label the different male types was deceptive. Because as I read, I quickly realized that underneath this humor, the labels were right on target and the descriptions were perceptive and accurate. In fact, I'd run across many of these different types of men myself.

This book had a great concept, a unique slant, and pragmatic content. As an entrepreneur, it is second nature to see the bigger picture, and I could see this book's potential. I was hooked on getting it out to a wider audience than the author had initially envisioned. And thus began my connection with the author to help get the book to press.

While the title might suggest that this book is solely for women, nothing could be further from the truth. Certainly women will benefit from recognizing themselves and their men on these pages. After they stop laughing, they can begin to assess who they are, why they get involved with certain male types, what patterns they see in dating and relationships, and how to unravel the mysteries of men. And for men, this book is equally beneficial. One way to better understand women is to discover how women perceive men. This book is a revelation, filled with information a man could only learn by listening in on women's conversations about the men in their lives.

There are literally hundreds of books written about dating and relationships, but there is only one *Dictionary for Women*. Yes, you will learn something new about yourself and your love life, but most importantly, you'll have a good laugh along the way.

CONTENTS

3-5 THEORY

The 3–5 Theory is one that suggests that it takes three to five different men to make up the equivalent of one perfect man.

A little girl grows up and pieces together this fantasy man. She gathers ideas from movies, books, the romantic things she's seen her friend's boyfriend do, the relationship between her mother and father, and even some outrageous thoughts she's managed to brew up herself. She fails to realize the following:

1. Books and movies are just that—books and movies!

2. Her girlfriend and mother probably think about leaving their men on a daily basis.

3. No man is perfect!

She's a woman now. Relationship after relationship has passed, and each has left her more disappointed than the last. She decides she's done with relationships. Only casual dating for her until someone worthwhile comes along. So she's dating four men currently. (She's not having sex with all of them, just dating.)

The first man is a blatant deadbeat. He has no job, no money, and no goals. But this is acceptable because his body is gorgeous, he's blessed below the belt, and his sex game is amazing.

The second guy is incredibly goal-oriented. He's educated, wealthy, and spiritual, and he's an overall nice guy. The problem is his swag. He has none! He's boring and can't keep her interest for more than an hour.

The third candidate is a die-hard romantic. He's older, likes to spoil his woman, and knows exactly what she needs to feel special—flowers, candy, jewelry, dinner, and vacations. All this is great, but the constant malfunction in the bedroom is definitely an issue.

And last but not least, there's "the friend," the one who's always there when she needs him. Whether it's changing a tire, hanging a picture in the house, or just giving her a shoulder to cry on, he's always there. But he's stuck in the friend zone. He's been there for about four years now, and it doesn't seem like he'll be moving anytime soon.

This woman wakes up one day and concludes that this is the happiest she's been in years. She can't really figure out how she could be so satisfied with her love life when she has no real commitment to any one man. She takes out a notepad and jots down the pros and cons of the four men currently in her life. She realizes that if she combines the positive aspects of all the men, she will find what she has been desperately searching for—her fantasy man.

The foundation of *The Dictionary for Women* is an elaboration of this 3–5 theory. This chapter contains brief descriptions of four types of men that women may encounter in their lifetimes. This handbook will go into the many juicy details about the varieties of men women have the pleasure of meeting, and it will also explore theories and terms that influence women's love lives.

What combination of men are you currently dating?

NINETY-DAY THEORY

The ninety-day theory states that not having sex with a man in the first three months of meeting him will give additional value to the relationship.

A woman is currently dating a man. This is their fourth date in the last month, and the evening is coming to an end. They are standing in front of her apartment door, and an awkward silence passes between them. The date went extremely well. The restaurant was perfect, and the conversation was great. He even brought her flowers and candy. He looked extremely good, standing in front of her, and the smell of his cologne teases her nose. He asks if he can come in for a glass of wine. She stands there in silence, debating her next move. He bites his bottom lip, squeezes out a seductive smirk, and leans in for the kiss. Her body melts in his arms, and the pulsating sensation between her thighs has made the decision for her. She's going to let him in. And it's definitely for way more than a glass of wine.

They have hot, passionate sex, and it is good! She kisses him on the lips the next morning as the sun rises. After her apartment door is shut and he's driving down the street, she jumps up and down for joy in the middle of her living room, still wrapped in her bedsheets. She's a kid on Christmas morning. She just found the perfect man.

At this point a few scenarios can take place.

Scenario 1: Destroy and Conquer

He never calls again. He's got the goods, and that's all he wanted.

His plan worked. She calls his phone about one hundred times—forty times from her phone, about twenty-five from her mother's number, another twenty-five from her girlfriend's cell, and a few blocked calls. Now she feels like an idiot, and he may have also labeled her a stalker. She's depressed and heading down the ice cream aisle in the supermarket.

Scenario 2: Let Her Sweat

He doesn't call immediately like she would have hoped. He's interested, but he's still playing the field. He still has other women to tend to. When he does finally call, she is super excited but tries to play it cool. In his eyes he's done nothing wrong. He's calm and collected, and it's obvious at this point that he probably is not ready to be in a relationship; however, he definitely wants to hang out and have sex from time to time.

Scenario 3: Who the Hell Are You?

He calls a couple days later. Both of them are excited, and it shows in their conversation. She comes to the conclusion that they should make their relationship exclusive.

She's only three weeks into the relationship when the true colors start to show. The romantic, caring, sexy, passionate man she first met is really a sweaty, lazy, ESPN-watching, cereal-eating fool who hasn't taken her on another date since she made it official.

Any one of the scenarios presented can be traumatizing. So this woman makes the decision that she will not allow any of these unfortunate matters to present themselves again. She will refrain from sex with a man for the first three months in order to get a true understanding of him as a person. She has also discovered that withholding sex sets a higher level of standards with men. He will pretty much give her anything she asks for during that time because he desperately wants to sniff the panties. From this point on, however, whatever he does for her in the beginning, she will expect him to always do for the remainder of the relationship. If he is not willing to wait, he probably isn't worth her time anyway.

Is ninety days too long to keep a man waiting? Yes or no? Why, or why not?

BABY DADDY
ˈbābē/ ˈdadē/

This man has several children by different women, and his lifestyle can be tremendously stressful and dramatic as a result.

AKA "my baby's father"

Synonyms: unreliable, dishonest, promiscuous

Pros

- Your child can play with stepsiblings.
- He may be a family man.
- His bloodline is definitely preserved for the next generation.

Cons

- You will have confrontation with other baby mommas.
- Your child may not get enough attention.
- He's probably at his other baby momma's house now.

This man is popular in today's society. You will see this species on an episode of *The Maury Show*, in the baby aisle at the market, or even in your own home. If this is your guy, be prepared

for drama. Keep your Vaseline and sneakers by the door, because the probability that you will have to whoop someone's ass
is exceptionally high. His other baby mommas will constantly
call his phone to complain about something their children need
or something you have done. It may be about clothes, money,
quality time, or why you grabbed her son by the shoulders
and shook his bad ass until he was dizzy. There will always be
something. If you want a man with a healthy savings account,
a baby daddy is not for you. After child support eats up his
paycheck, he can barely feed himself. Because he has kids with
these women, they most likely have attachments to him. You
can bet that he's still sleeping with at least one of them. Be
mindful that you may not know you have this type of man in
the beginning. Take a real good look at the kids around your
neighborhood. A couple of them may be his.

BUM BANGER
bəm/-'baNGər/

This man fails to stay employed and can't accomplish or set goals, but he is usually attractive, well-endowed, and extremely experienced in the bedroom.

AKA a bum who will bang your back out!

Synonyms: lazy, freeloader, uninspired, cheap, blessed, attractive

Pros

- He's entertaining.
- You're guaranteed to orgasm.
- He may be faithful.

Cons

- He's usually unemployed.
- He may ask you for money.
- He's unreliable (outside of the bedroom).

This man has managed to get through life without keeping consistent employment or doing anything of substance. As long as he is putting it down in the bedroom, he will always find a desperate woman in need of sweet satisfaction to take care of him. He has managed to perfect that thing called sex. It is so good that when he asks you to give him twenty dollars and to borrow your car, you cannot say no. He usually leaves you feeling drained, sweaty, temporarily disabled, and satisfied. Eventually this feeling wears off, and you realize you need to get more lunch money from the ATM, you have to be at work in fifteen minutes, and your car is still not in the driveway. In most cases, the bum banger is a younger gentleman who preys on older women (cougars).

CAUTION AUSTIN
ˈkôSH(ə)n/ ˈôstən/

This man falls in love with a woman during the premature stages of a relationship.

AKA "slow yo' ass down!"

Synonyms: too familiar, clingy, impulsive, trusting

Pros

- He's not afraid of using the "L" word.
- He likes commitment.
- He will give you the world.

Cons

- There's no chase involved.
- He's very persistent.
- He's a possible psycho.

You should be skeptical of this man. He wants the commitment, and he will tell you everything you want to hear. He will bring you lunch at work, give you flowers for no reason, and asks that you meet his mother. He may even have a couple conversations with you about marriage. The problem lies within the time frame. This is all taking place within the first couple weeks of meeting him. Therefore, you question several things.

1. How genuine are his actions?

2. Why you?

3. What's wrong with him?

4. Why the hell is he in such a rush?

Although women want all the affection this type of man expresses, it just seems too good to be true. And if this man is all he appears to be, why is he still single? Someone should have definitely scooped him up by now. So there are two scenarios that could speak to his bachelorhood. The first is that the relationship could lack the chase (see p. 87). This is a genuine guy, but women are complicated creatures. We desire attention from men, but when they give us all that attention at once, it feels boring and way too easy. Women like a process. We like to feel that we have worked to build the attention a Caution Austin will give right from the gate.

The other scenario is also very possible. He's single because there is definitely something wrong with him. He could be a stalker (see p. 85), ax murderer, substance abuser, woman beater, cross-dresser, premature ejaculator, etc. It is up to you to determine which one he is. If the developing relationship turns out to feed the latter scenario, run like hell. If it's the first scenario, get ready to go ring shopping! He is a rare breed.

CELIBACY THEORY

The celibacy theory suggests that a woman should take a vow to not have sex with any more men until she is a married woman.

A woman has just gotten married. It's been a frustrating two years, but she did it. There was no sex. There was some heavy-duty kissing, patting, and feeling, but nothing more than a PG-13 experience. Her friends laughed hysterically at her vow of celibacy in the beginning, and they doubted she would find a man who would go along with her plan. But she did, and he is great.

They are currently in their honeymoon suite in Hawaii, and things are getting hot and heavy. They have been waiting two whole years after all. He slowly removes the sexy corset she purchased for the special night. He kisses the back of her neck as her bra straps fall. He lies on top of her, and she gazes at his face under the flickering candle flames. A soft grin spreads over her lips. She's so pleased with the man she had chosen to marry. He enters her body for the first time, filling her up nicely, and she closes her eyes, preparing for the pleasure of his penetration. About a minute and forty seconds into the action, she hears a mighty growl followed by a satisfied sigh and panting. It's over. She opens her eyes to find her new husband exhausted, rolling over to his side of the bed. She lies there, confused and dangerously horny. She knew her stuff was good, but damn. *Maybe he was just excited*, she thinks. *He had been waiting a long time.* She's sure he will be ready for another round shortly, but before long, he's snoring.

It's the last day of the honeymoon now. And there has been some definite improvement. He's worked his way up to a whopping minute and fifty-two seconds! At this rate, he will hit ten minutes in a couple years. She had caught herself glancing at the attractive men on the beach during her honeymoon, fantasizing about a "long," passionate night of lovemaking. She feels guilty, but she wants so badly to be pleased. Did she make a mistake? If she had had sex with him early on in the relationship, would they still be on a Hawaiian honeymoon? She loved everything else about him, but this was going to be a problem. She relaxes on the beach and contemplates what will take place when they get back home.

Life could play out three possible ways.

Scenario 1: Sign the Damn Papers!

She could ask for a divorce and tell him that she made a mistake. There was no way she could be with a man who was already finished before she got her panties down.

Scenario 2: Sneakin' and Freakin'!

She could stay with him and cheat every chance she had with her ex, a broke dude from around her neighborhood. But what wasn't broke was his penis. He was Mr. Fix-It in the bedroom (see Bum Banger p. 11).

Scenario 3: The Four B's

She could stay with him and spend the rest of her life as a bitter bitch with plenty of bullets and batteries.

So is it realistic to not have sex with someone prior to the marriage? Even more important, is it smart? Now she may be stuck in an unsatisfying marriage, or she may look like a shallow bitch if she cheats or gets a divorce.

Why did she choose to be celibate in the first place? She wanted her relationship to be about growth, love, and understanding, not one based on sex like many of her previous relationships had been. But in the end, it still ended up being about just that. Well, the lack thereof in her case.

Which scenario would you choose? If you wouldn't choose any of the above, create your own scenario.

THE CELEBRITY

sə'lebrədē/

This man's fame and status keeps his counterpart emotionally exhausted.

AKA superstar

Synonyms: icon, famous, star, household name

Pros

- He has fame.
- He has wealth.
- He's attractive.

Cons

- He's not always available.
- He may have several women.
- He's unattached emotionally.
- He's arrogant.

This man is the singer, rapper, athlete, or actor you fantasized about. He's a "#mancrushmonday" type of guy. He's the man every woman wanted and knew they could never have. But you managed to lure him your way, and he easily seduced you into his superficial world. You've quickly become accustomed to the perks of his celeb status—the frequent jet-setting; the mansions in LA, New York, and Miami; the villa in Paris; the indoor garage that resembles a car show, and the endless cash flow available for whatever you desire. But you've also gotten a taste of the not-so-glamorous world of fame—the pestering paparazzi outside the restaurant during your dinner date, the sleazy tabloids featuring the worst photo they could find of you, the shady bloggers telling the world you're his newest whore, and the shameless groupies throwing themselves at your man on a daily basis. Although there are constant reminders that he has a girlfriend in every other state (and possibly other children), he makes you feel like you're the only woman in the world when you're together. But in the back of your mind, you know another contender will be waiting in the hotel at his next destination. When he's on the road, he's capable of turning his emotions off like a light switch, and he quickly transforms into the superstar he's known to be. You see him come across your television screen, and he's almost unrecognizable, no longer the sensitive, loving man who rubs your feet at night. He has an image to uphold, and unfortunately you aren't what his fans want to hear about. The money and gifts he provides as replacements for his presence give you momentary satisfaction, and you spend many nights alone or in the club with your friends, wishing he was there. Other men constantly hit on you, but they are never good enough. So what keeps you around? The high! You're celebrity man is a well-dressed drug you just can't kick. And that temporary fix he provides when he's around is enough to keep your blood boiling until he returns again. Endless love, a glamorous lifestyle, and un-bending loyalty have you holding on to this fantasy man. It's a dream when he's with you and a nightmare when he's away. But your heart is in it, and your mind is made up. And there's nothing the Internet, television, or anyone around you can say to change it.

CLUB CLINGER
kləb/ kling 'ər

This man purchases a woman a drink in a club, and then he is convinced he has the right to follow said woman around the club for the remainder of the night and possibly sleep with said woman at the end of the night.

AKA a cock-blocker

Synonyms: clingy, desperate, annoying, jealous

Pros

- You get a free drink.
- Maybe he buys you two or three drinks.
- He may even buy drinks for your friends.

Cons

- He's annoying.
- He's a potential stalker.
- You may have given him your real phone number.

This man is a pathetic being, and you can find him in any bar, club, or lounge. He will usually come off as charming in the beginning. You exchange phone numbers with him, and he buys you a drink. You're even considering actually calling him. You thank him and walk away from the bar. You move through the club, sip your drink, and dance with your friends. Suddenly you feel a groin rubbing against your backside and hot breath on your neck. You turn to find him, your club clinger two-stepping and grinning from ear to ear. You have two choices at this point. You can dance with him and allow him to buy you and your friends drinks for the rest of the night, or you can bob and weave through the club for the remainder of the evening until he gets the hint. In rare cases, a club clinger may become a boyfriend. You can read more about this under Stalker (p. 85).

CORPORATE CLOWN
ˈkôrp(ə)rət/ kloun/

This man is educated and a successful member of the corporate society, but his demeanor usually causes confrontation with his counterpart.

AKA an uncle tom

Synonyms: uptight, arrogant, white collar, obnoxious

Pros

- He's wealthy.
- He's educated.
- He's connected.
- He looks good in a suit.

Cons

- He's cocky.
- He's boring.
- He's too smart for his own good.

This man is extremely attractive. He will always wear the best from his cufflinks down to his socks. He will treat you well and buy you expensive clothes and jewelry, because his woman should always look good enough to be in his presence. He will take you to his boring business dinners, but he won't want you to speak, because his woman should know her place. No matter your level of education, you will never be as intelligent as he is in his eyes. He expects you to kiss his ass while he kisses the ass of his boss. As far as the bedroom goes, he's confident enough to get the job done, but he's too uptight to really put it on you. His superficial lifestyle may keep you around for a while, but when the Pradas and Christian Louboutins get old, you'll use them to walk right out of his life.

COYOTE UGLY
ˈkīˌōt,kīˈōdē/ ˈəglē/

This man is extremely unattractive, and women will not usually display their connection to him in public; however, he typically has something else of value, so a woman will keep him around.

AKA "you sho' is ugly … but"

Synonyms: ugly, bad teeth, bad skin, damn!

Pros

- He could be wealthy.
- He could be a good friend.
- He could be dependable.

Cons

- He's probably desperate.
- He's not attractive.
- He should not reproduce.

This man is definitely not a looker. He is usually insecure, but he hides it well behind one of many possible positives, including money, success, and/or a big penis. He may give good head, or he may have something he knows you want. This relationship usually begins accidentally—a drunken one-night stand, a dark club, a blind date from a social network, etc. He manages to lure you in with his other assets. You'll stay at the house for most of your dates. If you do go out, you go to a restaurant with dim lighting, or you frequent a late-night movie. He has not met your friends or family, and you have no intention of maintaining a long-term relationship. In rare cases, a coyote ugly may become a husband (see trick p. 95).

THE DADDY
ˈdadē/

This man is one of age and experience. He is fond of the younger woman, and he will spoil said woman with endless gifts with the expectation of receiving something in exchange.

AKA sugar daddy

Synonyms: old head, pop pop, gentleman, Hugh Hefner

Pros

- He's wealthy.
- He's a caretaker.
- He's experienced.
- He's charming.
- He will give you space.

Cons

- You don't have a lot in common.
- He wears dress socks in the bed.
- He may have a lack of stamina.
- He's usually married.

This man is usually a positive attribute in a woman's life. He is successful, and he has the investments and bank accounts to prove it. He has worked hard for his accomplishments, and now he wants to just enjoy his life. He doesn't accept his gray hairs very well, and he needs some form of excitement to stay young. That excitement usually comes in the form of a sexy young woman. The daddy most likely has a family. Don't be surprised if he has a son or daughter in your age bracket. He will fulfill all your financial needs, paying your rent, car note, utilities, etc. He will spoil you by buying you all the hottest designers. He will fly you to an extravagant resort on an island to enjoy a relaxing vacation. He doesn't think twice about his generosity toward you because he has the money to blow, you excite him, and he knows he is constantly competing against a younger, firmer generation. You probably are not extremely attracted to him physically, but you can fall in love with his charm, generosity, and courtship. In the bedroom, he will spend a lot of time on foreplay because once he penetrates you, sex won't be long before it's over. Overall, the Daddy is a good time. Just be mindful that he is married, and in most cases, he has no intentions of leaving his wife. You will always be the mistress. So play your role, stay in your lane, and enjoy it while it lasts.

"DIVIDE BY THREE" THEORY

The "divide by three" theory proposes that a woman divide her number of sexual partners by three before telling a man.

A woman is lying in the bed with her boyfriend. She's been seeing him for six months. They are watching a late-night TV show, and the topic is double standards. Number of sexual partners comes up, and her boyfriend turns to face her. She knows what's coming next, and she gets up to go to the bathroom before he can ask. While on the toilet, she contemplates the response she will give him. She knows he will definitely have the question on the tip of his tongue when she returns. She's thirty-two, and she's had sex with fifteen people, including him. She lost her virginity to her first boyfriend when she was sixteen. She's basically had sex with an average of one person a year. She's never had sex with another man while she was in a relationship.

Here's the breakdown:

- seven relationships,
- five friends with benefits, and
- three one-night stands.

She comes into the bedroom to find him anxiously awaiting her return. She lies down beside him and leans over to kiss his lips. The notorious question comes. She knows that her answer can make or break her relationship. She calmly states she's had five sex partners. He shrugs his shoulders, says okay, and rolls over to go sleep. He is obviously comfortable with the number, and he will sleep well tonight. But what if she had told him the truth? Would he have broken up with her? Would he have labeled her a whore?

Now let's take a look at his stats, which include

- four relationships,
- nineteen friends with benefits, and
- twelve one-night stands.

So he is thirty-six years old, and he's been having sex since he was fifteen. He has had thirty-five sexual partners. (Be mindful that thirty-five is a hundred in his mind.) His number of partners is double the amount of his girlfriend's. Almost 50 percent of her sexual partners were legitimate relationships, which runs contrary to his 11 percent relationship ratio. So who's really the whore? Who is he to judge?

But women will continue to live by the "divide by three" theory for fear of being judged, rejected, or ashamed because of that magic number.

What's your breakdown?

- Relationships = _____
- Friends with benefits = _____
- One-night stands = _____

What's your relationship ratio?

Number of relationships _____ ÷ total sexual partners _____ = relationship ratio _____ percent

Does it matter to you how many partners your boyfriend/ husband has? Why, or why not?

"DON'T NEED A MAN" THEORY

The "don't need a man" theory is one usually supported by an independent, successful woman who believes she does not need a man to complete her or to be happy.

A thirty-six-year-old woman has just gotten a promotion at work. She is a lawyer at one of the biggest law firms in town, and she has just made partner. She invites a few girlfriends over to celebrate her success. She sets up a delicious spread of exotic cheeses and wine by the pool in her six-bedroom luxury home. Her friends arrive, and they sit around the pool for hours, laughing and drinking. They congratulate her on all her successes, for they truly admire her strength and how she's managed to accomplish so much on her own. Two of her three friends are married, and the other has just gotten engaged. She is currently single, and she has no potentials in the running.

Let's take a look at the conversation.

Girlfriend 1: "You are too much girl. You have this gorgeous house. You look amazing, and now you're partner! What next? The first woman president?"

They all laugh.

Girlfriend 2: "I don't know how you do it, working all those hours. You need to take some time off to find a man! Get some love in your life."

Thirty-Six-Year Old-Woman: "As far as loves goes, I love myself more than anyone else can. And the last thing I need right now is a man. I don't need anybody adding extra stress, aggravation, or inconvenience to my life. Besides, what can a man do for me that I can't do for myself?"

Girlfriend 3: "I got something in mind ..."

Girlfriend 3 smirks. They all giggle.

Thirty-Six-Year-Old Woman: "I don't need him for that either. That's what my boo is for."

Girlfriend 3: "And who is your boo?"

Thirty-Six-Year-Old Woman: "You know ... B-O-O. My trusty battery-operated orgasm. He never disappoints me!"

They all laugh.

It's almost 9:00 p.m. now, and her girlfriends have to head home to their men. After they leave, she takes a bubble bath and crawls into her king-size bed to enjoy a relaxing night with cherry vanilla Haagen-Dazs and the Lifetime Channel. She thinks about the conversation with her friends. In their eyes she exuded confidence and happiness. But she's not happy. In fact, she's lonely. But there was no way she could display that openly with her friends. Was her nonexistent love life really her choice or just circumstance? She's a very attractive, successful woman, and she has certain expectations for the men she dates. But she would only really meet two types of men—men who were intimidated by her success and men who wanted to abuse it. It had been so long since she let anyone into her life. She would be surprised if she could remember how. Her throat tightens, and her eyes turn glassy as she tries her best to hold back tears. But they come tumbling down her cheek anyway, and she sobs into her pillow before eventually falling asleep.

So is the "don't need a man" theory really a deceptive persona put forth by successful women who have been previously hurt by men or those who have a hard time finding men? Or do some women truly believe that the love and companionship of a lifetime partner is not fundamental? You will notice that many successful women support this theory. Would it be safe to conclude that because a woman has money and a dildo, she no longer needs a man? Are men only good for money and sex?

Excluding sex and financial stability, name three things you need a man for in your life.

THE DREAMER
ˈdrēmər/

This man's indecisive and unrealistic approach to life goals frustrates his counterpart.

AKA daydreamer

Synonyms: unpractical, visionary, wishful thinker

Pros

- He's optimistic.
- He's multitalented.
- He's persuasive.

Cons

- He has no job, or he only works short-term jobs.
- He lacks commitment.
- He's a high flight risk.

The dreamer is a smart, talented man with plenty of skill and so much potential. But his best assets are also his greatest hindrance. He's a jack of all trades but a master of none. On your first date, his experience and well-rounded conversation will keep you interested. The places he's been, the people he's encountered, and his ambitious chatter about his preliminary career will have you on board and fantasizing about the empire you can build together. You move quickly into the relationship, boasting to your friends about how great of a man he is, defending what you believe to soon become your man's thriving profession. A year has passed, and lover boy is on his third *big break*. This time it's real estate, and he has the nerve to ask you to invest in his real estate license. A man who has big plans in life is something that every woman wants, but a man who can execute and provide is what every woman needs. What started off as a promising relationship has boiled down to nothing but smoke and mirrors. After a year of twists, turns, and new directions, you realize this is probably not going to work. Give this man an ultimatum and a job application. Don't be surprised when he tells you he's moving halfway across the country to pursue his new acting career.

FRAUD
frôd/

This man appears to have the materialistic items, lifestyle, or qualities a woman wants, but in all reality, he does not possess any of the assets a woman is looking for.

AKA stop frontin'

Synonyms: fake, phony, scrub, liar, dud

Pros

- He usually dresses well.
- He's charming.
- He's familiar with all of the designers.

Cons

- He probably lives with his mother.
- He drives his friend's car.
- He's a pathological liar.

This man is one to watch out for. You will see him leaning against a hot car as the night club let's out. He's usually attractive. His swag is priceless. He will be dressed from head to toe in designer wear. You will take notice of his watch, belt, and shoes, and you may be instantly impressed. You will give him your number, and you will anticipate his call. You've been on three dates now, and the truth is slowly unveiling itself. He's worn that same watch, belt, and shoes every time you've seen him, and you're pretty sure he's worn the same jeans twice. He's asked you to pick him up with some excuse about his Benz being in the shop. You've talked to him a couple times on the phone, and you keep hearing an older woman in the background. You will soon discover that this older woman is his mother and that he lives with her. No, wait. "She's living with me," he says. That Benz he keeps referring to is a 1989 260 E, and it's in the shop more than it's out. And you're pretty sure at this point that he had to put together about three months of his salary to purchase that watch, belt, and shoes. The Fraud usually will keep friends around who really have the qualifications he claims to possess. These friends help him keep up this fraudulent persona. By this point you're thinking that you got stuck with the dud. You ask yourself if people will think you're a whore if you move on to one of his baller friends. He will have his whole paycheck in his pocket on Friday afternoon and brag about how much money he has and the places he's been, but he will always have an entertaining excuse about why you've never seen him spend more than a hundred dollars. You will roll your eyes at his bullshit, and the day will go on.

FREAK BOY
frēk/ boi/

This man's strange and questionable sexual behavior or fetishes have the tendency to frighten his mate.

AKA "what are you doing back there?"

Synonyms: freak, nasty, kinky, WTF, OMG, why???

Pros

- He has sexual ability.
- He thinks outside the box.
- He loves every part of your body (every part).
- He's flexible.

Cons

- He has a lot of sexual partners.
- You can't kiss him on the mouth.
- He goes way too far.

This man is a "damn if you do, damn if you don't" kind of guy. You want a man who can give you a run for your money in the bedroom, but you also don't want to wake up shaking your head in regret about the ski mask, feather duster, and duct tape lying on the bedroom floor. Everyone, man and woman, has fantasies and fetishes, but when are things going too far? No woman wants to stop in the middle of sex to tell her man to move his finger, tongue, or other body parts from places they just don't belong. A woman doesn't want to shoot him a nasty look because his sex talk just got a little too kinky. The night can go from body-trembling orgasm to awkward silence really fast. That's not fun. This man just needs a little training. Meet him in the middle. There's nothing wrong with a little role-playing, dominatrix, or dirty talk. If you don't compromise, he will find another woman who will. Please believe that they are out there. So step out of your comfort zone a little bit, but make it clear to him what absolutely turns you off. He wants to please you. He'll listen.

THE FRIEND
frend/

This man will do all the chores and maintenance of a husband because he truly desires to be in a committed relationship with a woman, but he's unaware or in denial about the fact that said woman has no intention of ever being in a relationship with him.

AKA a sucka

Synonyms: buddy, flunky, pushover, homie, "brother"

Pros

- He's handy.
- He's reliable.
- He's generous.
- He's supportive.

Cons

- He's clingy.
- He's pathetic.
- He's unrealistic.
- He has no backbone.

This man is probably the sweetest man you will ever meet. He is not unattractive, but he lacks challenge and excitement. He will do anything you ask because he genuinely cares. He will maintenance your car, take out your trash, loan you money, fix things around the house, and walk on water if he could. You can usually talk to him about anything. Men hit on you in front of him, and he says nothing. You feel comfortable around him. You can even walk around in your panties in front of him and not think twice about it. But he will. He is lusting for you, dreaming at night, hoping that one day you will come to your senses and be his. But you never will. He will always be just a friend. And years from now, when he moves on and gives another woman the world, you will secretly regret not tying him down when you had the chance.

THE HEARTBREAKER
härt/ 'brākər/

This man has all the qualities a woman is looking for, but he refuses to commit to one woman.

AKA the player

Synonyms: the bachelor, single, promiscuous, undecided

Pros

- He's good-looking.
- He's financially stable.
- He's charming.
- He's good in bed.

Cons

- He's cocky.
- He will not give you the attention you want.
- He has too many women.
- He's misleading.

Every woman has encountered this man. He is everything a woman wants. He is extremely sexy, successful, and great in bed. The problem is that he knows it. He knows he can have any woman he wants, and he refuses to choose. Why should he when he can have them all? But no matter how many times he stands you up, doesn't call, or disappoints, you cannot leave him alone. And he will come in and out of your life, breaking your heart over and over again. Don't think that he does not like you because he does. That's why he keeps coming back. But he's afraid he will miss out on the next best thing if he commits to you. By the time this gentleman settles down, he will probably be close to forty. He's just having too much fun as a bachelor. It can be difficult, but the best way to get this man's attention is to not give him any. As soon as you think you've held out long enough and you want to call his phone, hold out a little longer. He'll call you.

THE HUSTLER

ˈhəslər/

This man's profitable career in organized crime and other illegal activities positively and negatively influence his counterpart.

AKA the boss

Synonyms: gangster, drug dealer, thug

Pros

- He's intelligent.
- He's hood rich.
- He's a provider.
- He's well known.

Cons

- His lifestyle can be unstable.
- He may have a lot of women.
- You may become involved in illegal activity.
- He may be flashy.

This is a man of audacity, status, and respect. He's a celebrity in the hood and a leader to his peers. And every boss needs a first lady to ride with him. If this happens to be you, be prepared to have an exciting and extravagant lifestyle. Don't be mistaken. Your residence will still be located in the ghetto or in close vicinity to the hood, for a hustler needs to stay close to business. The few who get the pleasure to step foot inside his house will discover it has all the luxuries of a Beverly Hills condo. He will give his family the world and spoil you with things other chicks can only dream of. But be careful. Many will love him, but even more will hate him. His lifestyle is dangerous and risky, and your strong attraction to his thug passion and fast money can land you in a whirlwind of trouble. You will do anything he asks to help your man stay on top. One wrong move and life can go from lavishness and thrills to orange jumpsuits and handcuffs.

JAILBIRD
jāl/ bərd/

This man's constant incarceration damages the relationship between him and his counterpart.

AKA "I'm not coming to see you!"

Synonyms: unstable, unemployed, trouble

Pros

- You always know where he is.
- "First day home" sex is great
- He's faithful (though not by choice).

Cons

- You'll see a high phone bill.
- He may change religions.
- He may change sexual preference.

The jailbird is a man of inconsistency. This will be a love-hate relationship. You love him when he's home and hate him when he leaves you. In the beginning, you will write him four-page letters and send sexy pictures on a weekly basis. You will be extremely faithful in the hopes that he will be home soon. After a few months, missing him turns into resenting him, and you will write an angry letter telling him so. If you go to visit, don't be surprised by the physical and mental changes—prescription glasses he doesn't need, a kufi, Malcolm X quotes, etc. You question his new look and way of life, and he tells you he's a changed man. He will ask if you have cheated on him, and you will shake your head no reassuringly. (It's not cheating if he's locked up.) He comes home. You have mind-blowing sex, but within three weeks you get the notorious late-night phone call from the prison operator. Telling your children that Daddy's away at school can only work so long. This constant abandonment will eventually grow old and you will move on. You'll still send him an occasional letter and a picture but nothing compared to before. Soon enough he will get the hint. Once he catches on, expect a nasty letter in the mail.

MARRIED MAN

'merēd/ man/

This man is in a dedicated relationship by law with a woman, but he commits adultery in order to pursue a missing component in his marriage.

AKA the dog

Synonyms: unsatisfied, sneaky, manipulative, selfish

Pros

- He has to go home after sex.
- He's good in bed.
- He can be blackmailed.
- You may not have to explain yourself.

Cons

- His wife will always come first.
- You may fall in love with him.
- He is for rent, not to own.

This is a man to avoid. In the long run, he will be a great disappointment. If you didn't know he was married when you met him, you will be very hurt, but you may be in too deep to turn away. If you did know he was married from the beginning, then you should prepare yourself for the worst. He will tell you many things to make you pity him and his horrible marriage—how he is so unhappy at home, how he's only staying around for the kids, how they don't even sleep in the same bed, how they haven't had sex in years. He will sneak you in and out of hotels on the other side of town, and if he has any class, he may whisk you off to a secret getaway out of the state. You will get an adrenaline rush just from the scandal itself, and the little time you get to spend with him is amazing. Eventually, you will become tired of coming in second and request that he leave his wife. He will tell you that he will leave her soon and continue to lie to keep you around for as long as he can. You'll either get pissed off and call his wife, continue to play the mistress, or in very rare cases, convince him to divorce her and marry you. If the latter happens, you'll soon discover that he was way more attractive and interesting when you didn't have to live with him, and now he's probably cheating on you with the new secretary.

MILITARY MAN

milə͵terē man

This man's life-altering experiences in the armed forces can have a damaging effect on his relationship.

AKA soldier boy

Synonyms: serviceman, fighter, trooper

Pros

- He has a great physique.
- He looks good in uniform.
- He's a provider (awesome benefits).

Cons

- He's away from home for long periods of time.
- He may have psychological issues after deployment.
- He may be physically aggressive and controlling.

You should be conscious of the military man. He is beautiful on the outside. His buzz cut, tailored uniform, assertive strut, and demand for respect will turn many heads. If he chooses you as his woman, be prepared for a thrilling ride. The military man usually craves commitment. Risking his life and experiencing close encounters with death have him yearning for love, family, and legacy. You will fall in love almost instantly. Marriage does not scare this man away, and a spontaneous trip to the justice of the peace may come quickly. Being a military wife can come with some great perks, including education financing, health insurance, housing assistance, and so much more. Staying on base with your husband can be interesting, but if you do, you must get used to the lack of privacy with his commanding officers so close by. When you're together, things are great, but if your man is headed out into battle, it can be such a scary time. Your phone will stay by your pillow at night as you wait for his call. You'll fear any late-night knocks at your door, praying it's not the dreaded announcement from a CNO (casualty notification officer). When he returns from war, be prepared for his emotional inconsistencies. His frequent gazes, night sweats, bad dreams, and heavy drinking can be overwhelming and cause some serious strain on your relationship. Don't be mistaken. He adores you, but adjusting to family life again can be a difficult process. If you have children, he will spend a lot of time catching up with them, mesmerized by how quickly they have grown in his absence. The military has made him an aggressive man. He is so accustom to the routine and controlled life of the military. He demands respect and control in his household. If you are not the meek type, your disagreements can quickly escalate, and his aggressive nature can be scary. It will take little effort to fall in love with the military man, but it will take lots of patience and understanding to maintain this relationship. Invest in some individual counseling for him and group therapy for the family if you want this partnership to work.

MOUSEWIFE
mous/ wīf/

This man hides at home while his wife works. He takes on the responsibilities of the house and children.

AKA man-housewife

Synonyms: yes-man, timid, a bitch

Pros

- You will always have a cooked meal.
- You can take out your frustrations on him.
- You can boss him around.
- He's faithful.

Cons

- He's dull.
- He has no backbone.
- You will have to fight his battles.
- He's shy in the bedroom.

This man is not very popular these days, but this group of men is rapidly growing in numbers. Your income is enough to support the family, and therefore, you have made the decision for him to stay home. On the plus side, the house will be spotless. There will always be a cooked meal on the table, and the kids will be bathed and in the bed by the time you get in from work. On the downside, it bothers you that he's a better housewife than you ever were, and this fact may also turn you off at times. There is no excitement in this relationship. As a businesswoman, you are extremely feisty, and you can appreciate a little pushback every once in a while—a raised voice, a thrown dish, maybe even a good choke hold. But none of that will happen with him. He is as timid as a mouse, and you are a feline with heels. He will always say yes to you, even when he disagrees, because he knows you can rip his head off. In the bedroom you will be the aggressor. He will want sex with the lights off, and he will worry more about waking the kids than pleasing you. He will whine from time to time; however, all he needs is a good slap across the face, and he'll be right back to his wifely duties.

NAPOLEON

nə'pōlēən/

This man is about four or more inches below the average height for a man, and he feels the need to compensate for his lack of height with a domineering demeanor and extravagant lifestyle.

AKA little man, huge ego

Synonyms: demanding, loud, flashy, crazy, tiny

Pros

- His height may be in his penis.
- He can eat it standing up.
- He can fit in your purse.
- He's fearless.

Cons

- His aggressiveness can seem crazy.
- You can't wear heels around him.
- You lose him in the club.
- You can't go to amusement parks.

B. Lyric

This man is a cute little guy. His enormous ego and endless swag make up for those tiny little hands and feet. Everything around him will be big—his house, his car, the G's in his buckle. Although he's on the shorter side, he is still extremely attractive. He is well groomed, and he smells good. His body is definitely in shape too. He will be aggressive toward you and others. He feels the need to prove himself. He will grip you up at the club and jump up to throw a right hook at the six-foot-two guy who tried to talk to you. His courage and cockiness turns you on. His shortcoming has made him creative in the bedroom, and he will find new and interesting ways to please you. He will give you whatever you ask for, but don't be fooled. He is no sucker. Don't do what he wants, and he will cut you off like the electric company after the third notice.

"ORAL SEX IS NOT SEX" THEORY (OSNS)

The "oral sex is not sex" theory suggests that engaging in oral sex with a man is an acceptable practice early on in the relationship and not equivalent or as consequential as the physical act itself.

A young woman is sitting around the table with her girlfriends, enjoying a relaxing lunch on a Saturday afternoon. She is currently dating a successful investment banker. They've gone out a few times recently. One friend sparks up conversation about her newest contender.

Girlfriend: "So what's going on with the investment banker? He is extremely cute."

(Notice that women will often refer to men by their occupation.)

Young Woman: "Good. Good. We actually went out on our fourth date last night! I really like him. Great conversation. Very focused. Passionate. He may be a keeper."

She smiles.

Girlfriend: "Okay, all that is fine and dandy, but did you have sex with him?"

They all laugh.

Young Woman: "Of course not! He is not ready for that yet! But I did give him head."

The key word here is *but*. The conjunction *but* is used to introduce something that contrasts with what has already been mentioned. But in this case, the young woman is completely contradictive in her statement. The question is this: What defines sex to a man? If men associate sex with pleasure and ejaculation, then in his mind he had sex. Whether it's oral or not, he's won. In regards to the ninety-day theory (p. 5) and the third-date theory (p. 87), if a woman performs oral sex in either probationary period, she has contradicted the principle of said motive.

So what is the motive behind the "oral sex is not sex" theory?"

The intention is driven by fear. A woman may fear that a man will not stay around for long without getting sex. So she thinks that by putting her face in his crotch, she can please him but maintain her self-respect because she did not lay down with him. The young woman mentioned here prides herself on the fact that she has only slept with five men in her life. So what if she has given head to fourteen men. That is completely irrelevant to the OSNS mind-set. Does this make her better than the next woman who has slept with ten men? What is an acceptable ratio of oral sex to penetrative sex? Does it even matter? Or is sex just sex?

What is your oral to penetrative sex ratio? What about your personality speaks to your number?

PENNY PINCHER

ˈpenē/ pin(t)SH/er

This man is financially capable of living a comfortable lifestyle but is extremely tight with his funds, and he often inconveniences his woman and family in the budgeting process.

AKA cheap ass

Synonyms: tight, economical, resourceful, saver

Pros

- He's strategic.
- He has a healthy savings account.
- He will manage the bills.
- He always has something for a rainy day.

Cons

- He's controlling.
- There aren't any shopping sprees.
- There aren't any spontaneous outings.
- You only see generic brands in the household.

This man can be a burden and an annoyance to any woman, especially one who is accustomed to or desires the finer things in life. He will make you go weeks without a TV just to catch the best bargain at the end of the month. He will argue with you in the market because you won't buy the dented soup cans. He would rather buy you extra socks than turn the heat past sixty-five degrees in the middle of winter. In all reality, as a couple, you will never be broke. He is a good provider, and he will always make sure that his family eats and has a roof over their heads. The downside is he will only give you the bare necessities and never indulge you with luxury.

He always has something stashed away for a rainy day, but it never rains hard enough for him.

PI

p i'

This man is insecure, and his accusations and suspicious nature can destroy the relationship between him and his counterpart.

AKA private investigator

Synonyms: FBI, detective, observant, untrusting

Pros

- He's protective.
- He will give you a lot of attention.
- He wants to be your best friend.

Cons

- He's too possessive.
- He won't believe anything you say.
- He may be cheating on you.
- He's pessimistic.

This man can cause strain and stress in any relationship he pursues. He will constantly question your whereabouts. He will call you several times throughout the day, and he always wants solid evidence to back up your answers. This untrusting mannerism usually comes from heartache in a previous relationship, or he may be questioning your motives because he's guilty about his own sneaky intentions. If a woman cheats on a man, that act can truly break his ego. Concerns about sexual ability or status can feed the insecurities of the PI. A man prides himself on his ability to please his woman in the bedroom. He would be devastated if you had sex with another man. But he may be just as distraught if you had an innocent phone conversation with a man who is more successful than him. Although he will want to know every move you make, he will not be open with you about his own actions. He believes he does not need to explain himself. If he simply doesn't trust women because of a bad situation in the past, try to hang in there. It will take some time for him to trust you. Once he does, the questioning will ease. On the other hand, if you have been around him every day for two years and he's still harassing you, start doing some detective work of your own! He may have something to hide.

THE POLITICIAN
ˌpälə'tiSHən/

This man is a political figure whose hectic and highly profiled lifestyle can be demanding on his counterpart.

AKA Mr. Mayor

Synonyms: elected official, statesman, public servant

Pros

- He's prestigious.
- He's a good talker.
- He's intelligent.

Cons

- He leads a busy lifestyle.
- He may be promiscuous.
- He lives life under the microscope.

This is a man of prestige. He is college-educated and goal-oriented. He makes a difference, and he's a networking genius. You were immediately attracted to his self-assurance, his upright stance, and firm handshake. Even though he is not the most attractive man in the world, his confidence is extremely appealing. The same finesse he used to win the people's vote will make you blush and smile from ear to ear. He will constantly be on the move, kissing babies, shaking hands, and looking for his next campaign sponsor. He may spend many of his days making public appearances within the community, and his evenings may be filled with business dinners and other political affairs. He is a brilliant man. And he and others will expect a brilliant woman to stand by his side. As the lady of a politician, people will constantly scrutinize your past dealings, level of education, wardrobe, and public speaking ability. You must always be dressed to impress with your finest knee-length skirt and pearls, caught up on all of your man's current political movements, and be prepared to make a thought-provoking statement on his behalf if you are stopped in public. Try to steer clear of the scandal, embezzlement, and political rivalry that can also come along with this expedition. Don't ask too many questions. Pay attention to large fluctuations in your bank account, and read everything he asks you to sign. Don't let the conservative and strenuous lifestyle this man leads in the public eye fool you. Behind closed doors he is yearning to loosen his tie and be himself. You're disagreements will be intense, and he will take out the stress of his workday on you. Your sex will be just as extreme, because the liberal inside him is a fervent man. As the old saying goes, he's looking for "a lady in the streets and a freak in the sheets." Keep this man happy with cooked meals when he's home for dinner, a couple of cookie-cutter kids, cerebral conversation, and mind-blowing sex. If you don't, when he makes it to the Oval Office, there will be a Monica Lewinsky wannabe waiting for him with a scotch on the rocks and a bib.

PRETTY RICKY

ˈprīdē/ ric i'

This man is very aware of his physical attractiveness, and this maintenance of his appearance resembles that of a woman.

AKA metrosexual

Synonyms: conceited, good looking, meticulous

Pros

- He's very attractive.
- He dresses well.
- He has a nice body.
- He will take notice of your outfit.

Cons

- He's uptight.
- He gets more attention than you.
- He may borrow your makeup.

Every woman likes a good-looking man, but we also appreciate the *manliness* of the man. We like guys who are a little rough around the edges, not dirty but rough. Pretty Ricky is the complete opposite. Every hair will be in place. His eyebrows may be arched. You may even take notice of a fresh coat of clear nail polish on his fingers and toes. When he's getting ready for a night out on the town, he will take longer than you to get dressed. And once you're out of the house, be prepared for him to stop and look at himself in anything that allows him to see his reflection. He can be naturally flirtatious in public because he believes every woman is drooling over him. More often than not, gay men will hit on him. You have even questioned his sexuality in the back of your mind. He is straight, but no woman wants a man who is prettier than her. This stylish gentleman can make his woman feel self-conscious about her own appearance. At night you want to be able to lay next to your man with no makeup and messy hair and feel comfortable, and you may not be able to do that in this relationship. You will always be part of what seems like an endless beauty competition. So if you plan to stay with Pretty Ricky, get over his looks, and just be yourself or you may need to stock up on the blush and hair gel, because he is always ready for the runway.

RAW MATERIAL
rô/ məˈtirēəl/

This man has all the assets needed to be a good catch but does not have the ability to put said assets to constructive use.

AKA "He would be cute if …"

Synonyms: geek, nerd, cornball, shy

Pros

- He's attractive.
- He's loyal.
- He doesn't get a lot of attention.

Cons

- He's shy.
- He's insecure.
- He's inexperienced.
- His ego may change in the middle of the relationship.

This is a man who has everything a woman needs. The problem is he doesn't know it. You meet him, and he's quiet and shy.

But you can see his attractive face right through the glasses, his muscular frame through his corny clothes, and a pinch of swag behind that lack of confidence. You take him under your wing, and he is intrigued and loyal. You talk him into contacts instead of glasses, a good teeth cleaning, and a trendy new wardrobe. You tell him how good he looks and show him a good time, building up his self-esteem. You do all of this to make him more attractive for you, but your plan backfires. Other women are giving your work of art more attention now, and it's obvious this newfound popularity is going to his head. His personality is changing. He's challenging your word and missing your phone calls. You've opened him up to a whole new world of fun, and now he's ready to explore. You can try your best to lock him down, because if you don't, he is sure to venture off to discover everything he's been missing.

SIMILAC

/sim' e lak'/

This man is entertained by child's play. He refuses to take on adult responsibilities, and he may have an abnormal attachment to his mother.

AKA momma's boy

Synonyms: immature, irresponsible, silly, adorable

Pros

- He is easily pleased.
- He's great with the kids.
- He makes you laugh.

Cons

- He's too playful.
- He's hard to have a serious conversation with.
- He has to ask his mother for permission.
- You will conflict with his mother.
- He has a fear of commitment.

Similac is a complicated man. The approval of his mother means a lot to him, and it can make or break your relationship. If his mother does not like you, the relationship will always have issues. It is usually hard to get this man to make any real commitments, especially when it comes to moving in together. He is comfortable living with his mother, who will wash his clothes, clean up behind him, and cook all his meals. If you are able to get him to move in, expect to pick up where his mother left off. If you can handle this, he will love you forever, but never as much as his mother. Most days, be prepared to lure him away from the PlayStation with some sexy lingerie or another entertaining act. The baby boy is usually fond of breasts since he's been on them his whole life. If you decide to reproduce with this type of man, he will be extremely close to his kids. Just remember that he is your biggest baby.

THE SQUATTER
ˈskwädər/

This man persuades his counterpart to allow him to stay in her home for a short period of time to try to establish a more permanent living arrangement.

AKA "it will only be a week or two …"

Synonyms: settler, dweller, unwanted resident

Pros

- He's charming.
- It's good sex.

Cons

- He's manipulative.
- He's messy.
- He's lazy.

The squatter seems to be a nice guy. He's not the most financially stable for one reason or another. (He's in between jobs, going to school, paying child support, or paying down a boatload of debt.) But your chemistry is amazing, and you decide to give him a chance. You've been dating for a few months now, and everything is going well. Lately you've been spending a lot of time together, most of it in the comfort of your own living room. You've enjoyed playing house, and the sex escapades over the last few weekends have been incredible; however, you still look forward to the freedom of being alone during the week. The things you take for granted like letting your boobs hang under your tank top, holding off on your shower just for the hell of it, and taking care of your morning breath close to the afternoon are now even more satisfying. But those privileges are no longer available. The squatter is a slithering snake looking for the perfect time to strike. You've just finished having body-trembling sex, and now is the time for him to go in for the kill. He spews out a long story about the issues with his current living arrangement and how he will only need to stay for a couple weeks. His doey eyes and chiseled chest have you in a trance, and you agree to let him stay. Three months have passed, and your squatter is in full bloom. Your comfy one-bedroom apartment is a wreck. Your refrigerator is empty. Your bathroom reeks of man, and your electricity bill is sky high. The honeymoon phase is over. You were not ready for this type of commitment, and you're starting to dread coming home at night. Unless you put your foot down, the squatter is here to stay. If you want to get him out, it's going to take some work—getting a restraining order, changing the locks, shutting off the electricity, calling a buff ex-con boyfriend, or star in your own psychotic episode. Meet up with your girlfriends, and over dinner, put your master plan into place. If you don't, say hello to your new common-law husband!

THE STALKER

'stôkər/

This man acts with obsessive behavior toward a woman of interest, which can cause her to feel extremely uncomfortable.

AKA psycho

Synonyms: crazy, weirdo, infatuated, creepy

Pros

- He's charming.
- He will give you a lot of attention.
- He will always be available.

Cons

- He's probably watching you now.
- He has rope and duct tape in his trunk.
- You'll have to change your phone number.

The stalker is a scary fellow. You will probably meet him in a place that you frequent often—a coffee shop, a gas station, a convenience store. He will ask you personal questions that he already knows the answers to. He will be sweet in the beginning, but the signs are usually there early in the game. He will gaze at you intensely over dinner to the point that you must look away. You may catch him freakishly sniffing your hair as you pass him by. You will wake up to text messages about how he's thinking about you, an abundance of voice mails that really don't say much at all, and some unsettling phone calls accompanied by heavy breathing and background noises. Every woman likes attention, but when is it just too much? Be careful when you are trying to break it off. Expect him to be sitting on the porch at your mother's house, pacing in the lobby at your office, and waiting outside the coffee shop where you first met. Take a self-defense course, and invest in a stun gun. He may need a good kick in the balls and some high-voltage action to get the point.

THIRD-DATE THEORY

The third-date theory suggests that a woman should not have sex with a man until after the third official date.

An official date is a planned outing that requires both parties getting dressed and leaving the house. The man should spend more than twenty dollars too; however, two official dates cannot occur in one twenty-four-hour period.

A young woman has probably had one real relationship since she's been dating. She's been on sixteen dates with ten different men in the last four months. She happens to really enjoy sex, and she has slept with nine out of the ten men she's dated. Lately she's been thinking a lot about this, and she realizes that at this rate she probably will end up having sex with fifty men this year! Her first date with lucky #10 is happening now. They are sitting in the car after seeing a movie, and he's all over her. He kisses her neck and rubs her thigh, and she's extremely turned on. He's cute as hell, and she can see the print rising beneath his jeans. She thinks about how good it would feel to ride him as she straddles him in the driver's seat. As he opens her blouse and runs his fingers over the lace of her bra, the thought of the fifty men she will sleep with this year rushes into her head. She stops this cutie in his tracks, buttons up her shirt, and insists he take her home. He pleads with her for about half an hour before giving up. He drops her off at her door and drives off into the night, hard, horny, and hopeless. She feels good about her decision and vows to continue to hold out with all her dates from now on.

So why did it feel so good?

It's because of a prominent term in the dating world known as "the chase."

The chase is the plan to keep a man interested by introducing a number of actions into a developing relationship, including but not limited to withholding sex, teasing, not answering the phone, ignoring him in public places, among others. It's a constant game of cat and mouse between men and women.

So why the third date?

On the first date, you've just met this man. You really don't know him from a can of paint. If you sleep with him now, what else is there? What if you had to put a price on your vagina? Is your vagina worth one dinner and a movie? It is now. In his eyes there's nothing else to look forward to. The main reason he's taking you on a date is to eventually have sex with you. Most men don't even expect to get any on the first date. So when you give him some, he thinks, *Wow, this was easy!*

On the second date, you've gotten a little bit more comfortable with him. There is still a little awkwardness, but you're making more eye contact. You're touching his shoulder at the dinner table, and his arm cups your back as you enter the restaurant. Your conversation about your previous date and late-night phone calls are entertaining and lighten the mood. If you haven't sized him up yet, you definitely are doing so now. You quickly glance at his crotch as you sip your wine. You giggle, and he smiles. He thinks you are laughing at his corny joke, but you're really blushing at the thought of his bedroom antics.

By the third date, let's face it. You're horny. That kiss good-bye from the second date had you all worked up. But it was nothing a hot bath, a glass of wine, and the trusty bullet couldn't fix! But you are way beyond the bullet at this point. You need the whole gun, the AK-47! Besides, he's done everything right thus far. He doesn't know, but you know as soon as you get into his car at the beginning of the date that you are going to sleep with that man. You nod and smile at his conversation and laugh at all his jokes while your panties moisten. He asks you if he can come inside, and you say no, allowing him to persist (which is all part of the chase). You finally give in and blurt out those infamous words, "Oh, what the hell. Come on in."

The third-date theory is one that directly contradicts with the ninety-day theory. When is it the right time for a woman to have sex with a man? In some cases, women marry the men they had sex with on the first date.

Do you see a pattern in the time frame that you give it up to a man? If so, why do you think this pattern exists?

"TICKET OUT THE HOOD" THEORY

The "ticket out the hood" theory proposes a woman should only entertain men of wealth and plot to get one of these men to marry her so that she can reap the benefits of his riches. This theory is usually supported by a gold digger.

A gold digger is a woman who dates men for financial and materialistic gain.

A young woman is standing alone in the VIP area at an exclusive, upscale nightclub in the city. She is dressed to impress, all compliments of her current situation (see Daddy p. 31). It's the album release party for a hot new artist, and the ballers are out tonight. She is a ferocious wolf of seduction, and she has already begun to stalk her potential prey. There's one in particular who has caught her eye. He is standing across the room by the bar. He's about six-foot-two, two hundred pounds. He's not very attractive, but he's distinguished and sexy. She quickly scans his *worth* by using her baller radar.

Baller radar is the ability to rapidly appraise a man's financial stature by observing his clothes, accessories, and other characteristics. This skill is one that does not come naturally, and it will strengthen with time.

Baller Radar Findings

- Armani suit ($3,200)
- Gucci loafers ($700)
- Rolex watch ($22,000)
- American Express Black Card (priceless)

Now it's time to execute her plan. She spreads another thin layer of Mac lip gloss over her lips, sprays a light mist of Burberry perfume, and smoothed her hands down her hips, ensuring her Calvin Klein mini was intact and just below the butt. She moves with a slow, seductive walk toward the bar. She stands close enough for him to get the remainder of the fresh Burberry vapor. She requests a martini from the bartender, pulls a fifty-dollar bill out of her Chanel clutch, pays for her drink, and turns to walk away, leaving him enchanted by her long, wavy hair, apple ass, and red-bottomed shoes.

(If you are confused about why she doesn't speak to him and instead walks away, please review section of the chase (p. 88).)

He's working his way through the crowd now, because at this point he is infatuated with her exotic look and mysterious manner. He finds her patiently waiting by the lower-level bar, and he kisses her hand. She smiles innocently and asks his name. They talk a little before leaving the club and heading to the five-star hotel, where he's staying for the weekend. She rides him that night like she has never ridden a man before. This is her lottery ticket out the hood, and he's holding the winning numbers! He moans loudly before releasing inside her. He kisses her forehead and goes to sleep. She lies awake next to him, a conniving smile across her face.

Mission accomplished! Consider the results now. She receives

- an 18.5-karat wedding ring,
- a mansion,
- two vacation homes,
- a cherry red Mercedes-Benz,
- endless shopping sprees, and
- two kids, which means guaranteed child support.

So why was her plan successful? Do not assume this is the first time she's executed a plan like this one. She has been working at this for years—cardio every day, teeth bleaching, weave extensions, three or four nightclubs a week, party-promoter connections, courtside NBA seats, etc. There is much maintenance and research that comes with the "ticket out the hood" theory. A woman who lives by this theory is one who understands men. She understands three very important components of a man's thought process.

The Visual

Men are very visual creatures. The initial attraction will be based completely on appearance.

The Physical

If he is attracted to a woman, he will want to have sex with her next.

The Residual

If the sex is good, he must then determine if he can financially, physically, and mentally afford to please this woman's request. If so, is the return on his investment worth the amount he must put out?

Therefore, this woman will understand that she must look good at all times, do the damn thing in the bedroom, and most importantly, set her standards early on. She will always have on the best when she goes out. This way, if she does come across a male caller, he will immediately know her taste level and expectations.

So is it wrong for a woman to go into a relationship with these intentions? Many women want a man to be financially supportive. But is there a difference between financial support and financial abuse. Is this woman truly happy with her man? Is the only bond with this man a monetary one? Money isn't everything. Or is it?

Should a relationship be fifty-fifty, or should the man be financially responsible for a larger portion of the relationship? Why, or why not? How should we break down this percentage?

TRICK

trik/

This man keeps a woman who would normally not be interested in him around by providing said woman with financial and materialistic contributions.

AKA "can you pay my bills?"

Synonyms: supporter, provider, desperate

Pros

- You will never be broke.
- You'll always look good.

Cons

- Be prepared to kiss his ass.
- You must always look good.
- His friends will label you a gold digger.

This is a man who will spend his last dime to keep you around. Do not confuse him with the daddy or another man of wealth. The daddy or another attractive wealthy man has the money to spend but most likely could still get a woman even if he didn't. The trick may or may not have a lot of money, but he will make sure you do at all times. He has low self-esteem. He may be unattractive or overweight. He was never the popular guy in high school. But he's watched a lot of rap videos or movies, and he has noticed that the popular guy always has the hot girl. Having a gorgeous girlfriend and being able to control her with money gives him power, confidence, and respect in his eyes. His friends and family will warn him about his choices, but he will not listen. As long as you look good on his arm, treat him well in the bedroom, and make him feel like a man, he will make sure you are well taken care of.

UNDERCOVER BROTHER

ˈəndər/ ˈkəvər/ ˈbrəT_Hər/

This man is in a committed relationship with a woman but will go outside of his relationship to get sexual satisfaction from a member of his same sex.

AKA down low man

Synonyms: gay, bisexual, denial

Pros

- He likes to have sex from the back.
- He may have good fashion sense.
- He will help do your daughter's hair.
- He has a nice body.

Cons

- He's dishonest.
- He's in denial.
- He may stop being attracted to you.
- He may have gone to jail.

This is a dangerous man. He is obviously a confused man. He has settled down and gotten married, and he may have a couple kids. He is not complete in his marriage, and he will go outside of his household to find sexual satisfaction with another man. He is in denial about his sexuality. This denial can develop in one of two ways. The man may be aware that he is bisexual, but he may be afraid that his peers or family will not accept him, so he lives a lie. This type of undercover brother has most likely always had these feelings since childhood but has tried his best to suppress them. The second form of denial is even more disturbing than the first. This type of man has sex with men (usually the giver) and does not identify as gay or bisexual. In his strange mind, this sexual act is one that is acceptable and cannot be defined. If you asked him if he was straight, he would proudly and convincingly say yes, not because he is a good liar but because he truly believes this. This undercover brother may be a six-foot-four, 250-pound, muscle-bound man who may have done some jail time. So keep your eyes open! Your brother may be under the covers with another brother.

DEFINITION OF A PERFECT MAN

Is there such a thing as a perfect man? That same woman who lives by the 3–5 theory will eventually grow restless and displeased with having to date three to five men to be happy. She will want to settle down, get married, and start a family with someone she can call her own. Finding a man who has everything she wants is unrealistic. Now that does not mean she should settle for anything, but she should make rational exceptions. Don't disregard a good man because he's not the right height, doesn't have the job you wanted him to have, or doesn't fit the exact mold of the fantasy man you've been creating since you started liking boys. Pay more attention to what really matters. Does he make you happy? We as women can get so caught up in the superficial, dreamy lifestyle portrayed in books, movie, and television that we may let great men slip right through the cracks.

The Dictionary for Women was not meant to put down men but to amusingly point out the positive and negative aspects of a variety of men we encounter and how we often maneuver through these interactions. We must all realize that there is no such thing as a perfect man, but there is perfect man for every woman.

Don't miss out on the perfect man for you!

On the following page, create your own definition of the perfect man.

My Perfect Man

Definition

_____

_____

_____

_____

Synonyms

_____

_____

_____

_____

Pros

_____

_____

_____

_____

Cons

_____

_____

_____

_____

Description

_____

_____

_____

_____

POP QUIZ

1. How many men does it take to make one perfect man according to one of the theories presented?

   a. 2–4
   b. 3–6
   c. 4–6
   d. 3–5

2. A man never calls after sex, and you call his phone several times. He never answers, and you get depressed. What is the name of this scenario according to the ninety-day theory?

   a. Let Her Sweat
   b. The Visual
   c. Destroy and Conquer
   d. None of the above

3. What man will need the approval of his mother before he makes a move?

   a. The Mousewife
   b. The Corporate Clown
   c. Similac
   d. The Jailbird

4. What man will you localize most of your dates to the house or a dimly lit restaurant?

    a. Coyote Ugly
    b. Caution Austin
    c. The Stalker
    d. None of the above

5. The ability to rapidly appraise a man's financial stature by observing his clothes, accessories, and other factors is ...

    a. The chase
    b. Gold Digger
    c. Official date
    d. Baller Radar

6. What is the motive behind the "oral sex is not sex" theory?

    a. Fear
    b. Horniness
    c. Peer pressure
    d. None of the above

7. Which is *not* a part of the three components of a man's thought process presented in the "ticket out the hood" theory?

    a. The visual
    b. The mental
    c. The residual
    d. The physical

8. Which man is tiny in size but big in personality?

    a. The Friend
    b. Napoleon
    c. The Baby Daddy
    d. The Undercover Brother

9. Which man is most likely to live with his mother?

    a. The Corporate Clown
    b. The Daddy
    c. The Fraud
    d. Caution Austin

10. The plan to keep a man interested by introducing a number of actions into a developing relationship is …

    a. The Ninety-Day Theory
    b. The chase
    c. The residual
    d. The Heartbreaker

11. What question could make or break a relationship according to the "divide by three" theory?

    a. What's your age?
    b. What's your weight?
    c. How many sexual partners have you had?
    d. Do you want kids?

12. Which man will you most regret not marrying?

    a.   The Married Man
    b.   The Heartbreaker
    c.   The Friend
    d.   The Penny Pincher

13. Which man has the most confidence when he has a gorgeous woman on his hip?

    a.   The Daddy
    b.   The Trick
    c.   The Corporate Clown
    d.   Pretty Ricky

14. Which man will have the most drama in his lifestyle?

    a.   The Baby Daddy
    b.   The Hustler
    c.   The Jailbird
    d.   The Fraud

WORD SEARCH

```
V T G D I R C W C O T L Y J E I M O F T W T N E O
N I V G S E X A P L H H R Y G L C P R S W U W T R
P C I D U H U D U T U W I W J B H E Y K K D O V A
R K A F G T U U B T O B P R N M H J F X N E L W L
C E Z L Y O I J Q W I N C F D C F R C Y C U C Q S
K T S V E R B E J A O O V L N D A Z C R L Z E H E
P O H T P B D F A Y X W N I I U A A R M A H T Z X
W U E I R R V N O R P N P A D N B T I C L R A U I
X T O E A E J Z E T H Y W B U I G S E B G W R L S
W T Z J G V T N M I N V R P L S P E L O W O O B N
P H J S L O Z K N N R O R E S C T R R O E Q P A O
Q E I Y H C D K E E A F C O T R J I Z N K G R B T
P H G Z U R M P K D H R P Z C Z W A N S Y L O Y S
U O B I L E N A P O L E O N D Y N A M I T E C D E
X O T M O D E E R H T Y B E D I V I D Y F Y P A X
M D H I E N N A M A D E E N T N O D L R I X J D Q
J O M Y B U N A M D E I R R A M Y G E H T U V D Q
A S U F J U Y D D A D J I G Y V U A M I H A P Y K
I C I S X I M D N A B U E N D E K Z I X Y F C S M
L X F M E U E B M Y L U B E T B R E K L A T S D V
B U U H I W Y G A H F S E O O W T T K N W C J Y P
I D U H A L I X T N X S Y Y P R E T T Y R I C K Y
R E G A C I A F I H G O U V Z B R Y T R N R A Y P
D V K E A U J C E Z C E L W D Y I N T U X J N Q Z
R E K A E R B T R A E H R T U S L M O Y M P V J R
```

Baby Daddy	Fraud
Bum Banger	Freak Boy
Caution Austin	Friend
Celibacy	Heartbreaker
Club Clinger	Jailbird
Corporate Clown	Married Man
Coyote Ugly	Mousewife
Daddy	Napoleon
Divide by Three	Oral Sex Is Not Sex
Don't Need a Man	

WORD SCRAMBLE

Unscramble the following words:

1. dadyd _____

2. iirbjdla _____

3. nantuacitousi _____

4. aririoetvntgitvape _____

5. brmbneagu _____

6. cugericnllb _____

7. tearskl _____

8. yaddybdab _____

9. onarctcrooplew _____

10. ruadf _____

11. aloonenp _____

12. cmilais _____

13. weisfueom _____

B. Lyric

14. robfayke _____

15. oltcugeyyo _____

16. nrmamdirea _____

17. hnnepenyripc _____

18. ekaebahrtrer _____

19. ycktyertrpi _____

20. erdetunverohcbror _____

21. alceybci _____

22. eaddhttir _____

23. ybddevrihitee _____

24. lxosrae _____

ABOUT THE AUTHOR

B. Lyric is a talented author, poet, song writer, and motivational speaker from Philadelphia, Pennsylvania who has been writing since the age of nine. She enjoys writing most about love, relationships, real women issues, and spiritual inspiration. Her biggest hobby outside of writing is spending time with her amazing husband and beautiful baby girl.

When B. Lyric decided to write The Dictionary for Women, she had an anthem for women everywhere in mind. She noticed that men and love seemed to always be a hot topic around her and she had spent so much time talking about the good, the bad, and the ugly of relationships with her friends and family. They had laughed and cried over their male troubles several times throughout the years and she truly believed there was a story that needed to be told. Not just the story of herself and those close to her but the story of so many women in America that had experienced something similar to what the women around her were going through. She wanted to give her readers something that would not only make them reminisce and ponder over past and present relationships, but also laugh along the way over the things that many women say amongst themselves but don't have the guts to say aloud. A book that would make women feel like they were talking to a best friend or make them pick up the phone to call them. She was so invested in collecting the biggest sample of opinions from real women, that her interviewing began to exceed her friends and family and venture out amongst various women she would encounter. She excitedly jotted down experience after experience until she had enough documented to create what is now *The Dictionary for Women*.

B. Lyric does not intend for the book to bash all men but humorously poke fun at real life situations. In fact, she admits that writing this book helped her to realize what a good man truly is and is partially responsible for the great relationship she has with her husband. She truly hopes her readers enjoy the book and all the laughs, questions, and conversation it has to offer.

Follow B.Lyric on her journey at
www.TheDictionaryforWomen.com

Printed in the United States
By Bookmasters